# Questions You'll Wish You Asked

## A TIME CAPSULE JOURNAL FOR
## GRANDMOTHERS AND GRANDCHILDREN

## Melissa Pennel

Follow Your Fire Publishing

Sacramento, CA.

Melissa Pennel / Follow Your Fire Publishing
FollowYourFireCoaching.com
Sacramento, CA.

Ordering Information:
Quantity sales: Special discounts are available on quantity purchases by corporations, associations, and others. For details, contact the publisher at the address above.

Questions You'll Wish You Asked: A Time Capsule Journal for Grandmothers and Grandchildren, Melissa Pennel — 1st ed.

ISBN 978-1-956446-00-5

*This journal belongs to*

_____

_____

_____

_____

May these pages be a sacred means of time traveling,
a talisman of connection and healing,
and a reminder that every story matters.

# CONTENTS

INTRODUCTION ..................................................................IX

YOUR YOUTH ....................................................................1

OUR FAMILY .....................................................................25

ON MOTHERHOOD AND GRANDMOTHERHOOD .......................45

ON WORK ..........................................................................67

ON LOVE ...........................................................................74

YOUR SPIRITUAL LIFE ........................................................87

KNOWING YOU BETTER ......................................................95

LIFE'S TOUGH MOMENTS ....................................................115

ON SAYING GOODBYE ........................................................123

ADDITIONAL QUESTIONS TO EACH OTHER ............................131

ABOUT THE AUTHOR ........................................................144

Discover more

# Questions You'll Wish You Asked

## Journals

**A Time Capsule Journal for Mothers and Daughters**

✢✢

**A Time Capsule Journal for Mothers and Sons**

✢✢

**A Time Capsule Journal for Fathers and Daughters**

✢✢

**A Time Capsule Journal for Fathers and Sons**

✢✢

**A Time Capsule Journal for Parents and Children**

✢✢

**A Time Capsule Journal for Grandparents
and Grandchildren**

✢✢

**A Time Capsule Journal for Grandfathers
and Grandchildren**

Learn more at FollowYourFireCoaching.com

*For Hazel, Rose, and Sha Sha*

# Introduction: A Note to Grandmothers and Grandchildren

The "Questions You'll Wish You Asked" journaling book series was born from a place of deep grief.

In the span of only a few years I lost three grandparents, my mom died of a heart attack, and my only remaining elder succumbed to dementia, dying soon after.

I was left in shock at the empty space where my family used to be.

*What do I do now?*

Though I shared endless conversations with these loved ones while they were alive, there were so many questions I had once they were gone—things I wish I asked, answers I didn't remember, and information that I craved.

*Who were they before I knew them?*
*How did their story shape mine?*
*What had they wanted me to know?*

Since that period of deep loss, I've often encouraged others to ask their loved ones the questions they might someday have. I believe the benefit is twofold: a deeper understanding of that person while they're alive, and a legacy to look back on once they're gone.

An unexpected gift of these journals are the meaningful stories that have poured in not just from the recipients, but from those writing down their story. These accounts of self-understanding, intergenerational connection, and unexpected healing have reinforced two things I've always believed to be true:

1.) Every story matters.
2.) Writing is a miraculous means to time travel, understand, and heal.

A mother now myself, I don't know if my kids will crave this information as I did—but just in case they someday do, I created the "Questions You'll Wish You Asked" journal series.

I created it for you, too.

Whether bound by blood or any other form of family, I hope these questions open conversations, soften inevitable struggles, and foster moments of intimacy that will be treasured for years to come.

Don't wait to ask these questions or fill out answers; jot some notes down now, and as the years go on feel free to add additional thoughts.

Let these words create an altar where you may visit each other in the future—because however far away it seems now, the time will come for all of us when conversation is no longer possible.

I hope this journal becomes a treasured keepsake that forever reminds you of the sacred and foundational bond that lies between grandmothers and grandchildren.

I hope it reminds you of the divine altar you already stand at: that which binds love across time and space.

*In love and gratitude,*
*Melissa Pennel*

# Your Youth

# What is your earliest memory?

_____

_____

_____

_____

_____

_____

_____

_____

_____

_____

_____

_____

_____

_____

_____

_____

**Do you know how your parents chose your name? Does it have a special meaning?**

_____

_____

_____

_____

_____

_____

_____

_____

_____

_____

_____

_____

_____

_____

_____

_____

_____

**Can you remember your childhood home? Can you describe the way it looked, the things you did there, and how it felt to be within it?**

_____

_____

_____

_____

_____

_____

_____

_____

_____

_____

_____

_____

_____

_____

_____

_____

_____

_____

## What was summer like when you were a kid?

_____

_____

_____

_____

_____

_____

_____

_____

_____

_____

_____

_____

_____

_____

_____

_____

**Did you have any irrational childhood fears?**
**Do you remember how you got over them?**

_____

_____

_____

_____

_____

_____

_____

_____

_____

_____

_____

_____

_____

_____

_____

_____

_____

## Did you have a secret hiding place as a child? Where was it?

_____

_____

_____

_____

_____

_____

_____

_____

_____

_____

_____

_____

_____

_____

_____

_____

_____

_____

## What are some favorite holiday memories?

# What did you most struggle with as a child?

## Who did you look up to as a child?

## Who were your childhood friends?
## What are some dear memories of them?

_____

_____

_____

_____

_____

_____

_____

_____

_____

_____

_____

_____

_____

_____

_____

_____

_____

_____

## Did you have childhood pets?
## What do you remember about them?

_____

_____

_____

_____

_____

_____

_____

_____

_____

_____

_____

_____

_____

_____

_____

_____

## What big differences do you see between how your generation was raised versus today's generation?

_____

_____

_____

_____

_____

_____

_____

_____

_____

_____

_____

_____

_____

_____

_____

_____

_____

_____

# What was a dream you had as a child?

_____

_____

_____

_____

_____

_____

_____

_____

_____

_____

_____

_____

_____

_____

_____

_____

## Was there a trip you took as a child that stands out to you? Why?

_____

_____

_____

_____

_____

_____

_____

_____

_____

_____

_____

_____

_____

_____

_____

_____

_____

_____

## What type of music did your parents listen to? Did you like it?

_____

_____

_____

_____

_____

_____

_____

_____

_____

_____

_____

_____

_____

_____

_____

_____

# Was there a particular chore you loathed as a kid? Why was it so bothersome?

_____

_____

_____

_____

_____

_____

_____

_____

_____

_____

_____

_____

_____

_____

_____

_____

_____

**If you could change one thing about
your childhood, what would it be?**

**What are your siblings' names? Did you get along? If an only child, did you ever wish for siblings?**

**Did you ever get in really big trouble as a teen? What were the consequences?**

_____

_____

_____

_____

_____

_____

_____

_____

_____

_____

_____

_____

_____

_____

_____

# What did you do for fun as a teen?

_____

_____

_____

_____

_____

_____

_____

_____

_____

_____

_____

_____

_____

_____

_____

_____

# Did you feel like you fit in as a teenager?
## Why or why not?

_____

_____

_____

_____

_____

_____

_____

_____

_____

_____

_____

_____

_____

_____

_____

_____

**If your teen years were a movie, what was the theme? Who were the main characters? Was there a sweetheart or a villain?**

_____

_____

_____

_____

_____

_____

_____

_____

_____

_____

_____

_____

_____

_____

_____

_____

**If you could give your eighteen-year-old
self a piece of advice, what would it be?**

_____

_____

_____

_____

_____

_____

_____

_____

_____

_____

_____

_____

_____

_____

_____

_____

# Our Family

## What are the biggest lessons you learned from your mother?

_____

_____

_____

_____

_____

_____

_____

_____

_____

_____

_____

_____

_____

_____

_____

# What are the biggest lessons you learned from your father?

_____

_____

_____

_____

_____

_____

_____

_____

_____

_____

_____

_____

_____

_____

_____

_____

_____

## What was your favorite thing about your mother? What about her did you struggle with?

_____

_____

_____

_____

_____

_____

_____

_____

_____

_____

_____

_____

_____

_____

_____

_____

_____

## What was your favorite thing about your father? What about him did you struggle with?

_____

_____

_____

_____

_____

_____

_____

_____

_____

_____

_____

_____

_____

_____

_____

_____

# Is there anyone in your family that you wish you'd been closer with?

_____

_____

_____

_____

_____

_____

_____

_____

_____

_____

_____

_____

_____

_____

_____

_____

What were your grandparents' names?
What words come to mind when
you think of each one?

_____

_____

_____

_____

_____

_____

_____

_____

_____

_____

_____

_____

_____

_____

_____

_____

_____

# Where was your mother's family from? Do you remember any stories they told about that place?

_____

_____

_____

_____

_____

_____

_____

_____

_____

_____

_____

_____

_____

_____

_____

_____

## Where was your father's family from? Do you remember any stories they told about that place?

_____

_____

_____

_____

_____

_____

_____

_____

_____

_____

_____

_____

_____

_____

_____

_____

_____

How do you think your mother's upbringing
shaped who she was? Do you think it
shaped the way she raised you?

_____

_____

_____

_____

_____

_____

_____

_____

_____

_____

_____

_____

_____

_____

_____

_____

How do you think your father's upbringing shaped who he was? Do you think it shaped the way he raised you?

_____

_____

_____

_____

_____

_____

_____

_____

_____

_____

_____

_____

_____

_____

_____

_____

**Is there any family lore that was passed down to you through stories? Maybe we had a famous ancestor, or mysterious scandal?**

_____

_____

_____

_____

_____

_____

_____

_____

_____

_____

_____

_____

_____

_____

_____

## Is there anything I should know about our family's medical history?

_____

_____

_____

_____

_____

_____

_____

_____

_____

_____

_____

_____

_____

_____

_____

_____

_____

**What can you share about our family's mental health history? Has anyone struggled with addiction, alcoholism, depression, etc?**

_____

_____

_____

_____

_____

_____

_____

_____

_____

_____

_____

_____

_____

_____

_____

_____

_____

## What was your mom's relationship with her mom like? What about with her dad?

_____

_____

_____

_____

_____

_____

_____

_____

_____

_____

_____

_____

_____

_____

_____

_____

_____

# What was your dad's relationship with his dad like? What about with his mom?

_____

_____

_____

_____

_____

_____

_____

_____

_____

_____

_____

_____

_____

_____

_____

_____

_____

## What is something you learned from the generations before you?

_____

_____

_____

_____

_____

_____

_____

_____

_____

_____

_____

_____

_____

_____

_____

_____

_____

_____

## What is something about our heritage that you want future generations to know?

_____

_____

_____

_____

_____

_____

_____

_____

_____

_____

_____

_____

_____

_____

_____

_____

**Is there a relative who passed young or before I was born that you wish I'd known? What would you like to share with me about them?**

_____

_____

_____

_____

_____

_____

_____

_____

_____

_____

_____

_____

_____

_____

_____

_____

_____

**What was something that your parents found really important to teach you? Why do you think it was so important to them?**

# On Motherhood and Grandmotherhood

**How did you know you were ready to have kids? If you could go back, would you have waited longer, or started having kids sooner?**

_____

_____

_____

_____

_____

_____

_____

_____

_____

_____

_____

_____

_____

_____

_____

_____

## What do you remember about your own pregnancy and childbirth?

# What do you remember about the
## day my parent was born?

## What was difficult about early motherhood? What did you love about it?

_____

_____

_____

_____

_____

_____

_____

_____

_____

_____

_____

_____

_____

_____

_____

_____

_____

**If you could change one thing about how you raised my parent, what would it be? What about how you parented them makes you proud?**

_____

_____

_____

_____

_____

_____

_____

_____

_____

_____

_____

_____

_____

_____

_____

_____

_____

# How did becoming a mother change you?

_____

_____

_____

_____

_____

_____

_____

_____

_____

_____

_____

_____

_____

_____

_____

_____

_____

_____

**Did you feel supported as a young mother? How could you have been more supported during this time?**

_____

_____

_____

_____

_____

_____

_____

_____

_____

_____

_____

_____

_____

_____

_____

_____

_____

## What are some special memories you have of my parent when they were young?

_____

_____

_____

_____

_____

_____

_____

_____

_____

_____

_____

_____

_____

_____

_____

_____

_____

# How did it feel to find out you were going to be a grandmother?

_____

_____

_____

_____

_____

_____

_____

_____

_____

_____

_____

_____

_____

_____

_____

# What do you remember about our first meeting?

## What are your favorite parts of being a grandmother?

_____

_____

_____

_____

_____

_____

_____

_____

_____

_____

_____

_____

_____

_____

_____

## What is something that has surprised you about being a grandmother?

## What are the biggest differences between being a mother and being a grandmother? What is easier, and what is more difficult?

_____

_____

_____

_____

_____

_____

_____

_____

_____

_____

_____

_____

_____

_____

_____

_____

**What do you hope I do differently in life than you did? What do you hope I do similarly?**

## What are your favorite qualities about me?

**What quality do you most hope I inherit from you? Is there anything you hope I will *not* inherit from you? Why?**

_____

_____

_____

_____

_____

_____

_____

_____

_____

_____

_____

_____

_____

_____

_____

_____

_____

## What advice would you give me about raising my own children?

_____

_____

_____

_____

_____

_____

_____

_____

_____

_____

_____

_____

_____

_____

# What are some things that you hope I experience in life? Why?

_____

_____

_____

_____

_____

_____

_____

_____

_____

_____

_____

_____

_____

_____

_____

_____

# What is a treasured memory you share of us?

_____

_____

_____

_____

_____

_____

_____

_____

_____

_____

_____

_____

_____

_____

_____

_____

_____

**What are you most proud of my parent for?**
**What are you most proud of me for?**

_____

_____

_____

_____

_____

_____

_____

_____

_____

_____

_____

_____

_____

_____

_____

_____

_____

_____

**If you could make one wish for my life,
what would it be?**

_____

_____

_____

_____

_____

_____

_____

_____

_____

_____

_____

_____

_____

_____

_____

# On Work

When asked "what do you want to be when you grow up?" as a child, what did you say?

_____

_____

_____

_____

_____

_____

_____

_____

_____

_____

_____

_____

_____

_____

_____

Did you work outside the home before or after kids? What was that experience like? Is there anything you would go back and change about your choices?

_____

_____

_____

_____

_____

_____

_____

_____

_____

_____

_____

_____

_____

_____

_____

_____

**What jobs did you have when you were young?**
**How did they shape who you later became?**

_____

_____

_____

_____

_____

_____

_____

_____

_____

_____

_____

_____

_____

_____

_____

**How did your parents make a living? What about your grandparents? Do you know what our distant ancestors did for work?**

_____

_____

_____

_____

_____

_____

_____

_____

_____

_____

_____

_____

_____

_____

_____

**Is there a job you always fantasized about
but never did? Why was it so appealing?**

_____

_____

_____

_____

_____

_____

_____

_____

_____

_____

_____

_____

_____

_____

_____

_____

## What are some ideas you want to pass on to me about work?

_____

_____

_____

_____

_____

_____

_____

_____

_____

_____

_____

_____

_____

_____

_____

_____

# On Love

# Do you remember your first date?
## What was it like?

_____

_____

_____

_____

_____

_____

_____

_____

_____

_____

_____

_____

_____

_____

_____

_____

## How did you meet my grandfather?
## What was your first impression?

_____

_____

_____

_____

_____

_____

_____

_____

_____

_____

_____

_____

_____

_____

_____

_____

**How did you know that you were ready to get married? Did you have any doubts? If so, how did you move through them?**

# What do you remember about your wedding day?

How has dating changed since you were young?
Do you think it's easier or harder now? Why?

_____

_____

_____

_____

_____

_____

_____

_____

_____

_____

_____

_____

_____

_____

_____

_____

_____

# What advice would you give me about relationships?

_____

_____

_____

_____

_____

_____

_____

_____

_____

_____

_____

_____

_____

_____

_____

_____

_____

# What have you learned about yourself from being in love?

_____

_____

_____

_____

_____

_____

_____

_____

_____

_____

_____

_____

_____

_____

_____

_____

_____

## What was your toughest breakup like? What did it teach you?

_____

_____

_____

_____

_____

_____

_____

_____

_____

_____

_____

_____

_____

_____

_____

_____

_____

**Was there someone you thought you would end up with but didn't? How did you handle that heartbreak?**

_____

_____

_____

_____

_____

_____

_____

_____

_____

_____

_____

_____

_____

_____

_____

_____

_____

How have your ideas about relationships
changed as you've gotten older?

_____

_____

_____

_____

_____

_____

_____

_____

_____

_____

_____

_____

_____

_____

_____

_____

_____

# What do you want me to look for in a partner?

## What do you believe are keys to a healthy, long-term, relationship?

_____

_____

_____

_____

_____

_____

_____

_____

_____

_____

_____

_____

_____

_____

_____

# Your Spiritual Life

**Did you have a relationship with God or a Higher Power in childhood? How did you form it?**

_____

_____

_____

_____

_____

_____

_____

_____

_____

_____

_____

_____

_____

_____

_____

_____

_____

_____

# Did your family have any religious traditions?

**As a child, what was your idea of God? How does that compare to your idea of God today?**

_____

_____

_____

_____

_____

_____

_____

_____

_____

_____

_____

_____

_____

_____

_____

_____

# What would you like to teach me about God?

_____

_____

_____

_____

_____

_____

_____

_____

_____

_____

_____

_____

_____

_____

_____

# Have you had any spiritual experiences that are especially sacred to you?

_____

_____

_____

_____

_____

_____

_____

_____

_____

_____

_____

_____

_____

_____

_____

_____

# Where do you connect the most with your spirituality?

_____

_____

_____

_____

_____

_____

_____

_____

_____

_____

_____

_____

_____

_____

_____

# Knowing You Better

## What are some of your favorite books and movies? Why do you love them?

_____

_____

_____

_____

_____

_____

_____

_____

_____

_____

_____

_____

_____

_____

_____

# Where are some of the places you have lived in life? Which was your favorite? Why?

_____

_____

_____

_____

_____

_____

_____

_____

_____

_____

_____

_____

_____

_____

## What are you insecure about? Do you know where this came from?

_____

_____

_____

_____

_____

_____

_____

_____

_____

_____

_____

_____

_____

_____

_____

_____

## Do you have an embarrassing moment that stands out to you? How did you recover?

_____

_____

_____

_____

_____

_____

_____

_____

_____

_____

_____

_____

_____

_____

# What is something you love about yourself?

_____

_____

_____

_____

_____

_____

_____

_____

_____

_____

_____

_____

_____

_____

_____

_____

# Is there something that people often get wrong about you?

_____

_____

_____

_____

_____

_____

_____

_____

_____

_____

_____

_____

_____

_____

# What is something that always makes you smile?

# What have you learned from friendship?

_____

_____

_____

_____

_____

_____

_____

_____

_____

_____

_____

_____

_____

_____

_____

**What is an ordinary moment from your day that makes you feel extremely grateful?**

_____

_____

_____

_____

_____

_____

_____

_____

_____

_____

_____

_____

_____

_____

_____

_____

# Where are your favorite places to travel? Why?

_____

_____

_____

_____

_____

_____

_____

_____

_____

_____

_____

_____

_____

_____

_____

**Are there any points in your life that you completely changed course? How did they change you?**

_____

_____

_____

_____

_____

_____

_____

_____

_____

_____

_____

_____

_____

_____

_____

_____

# What do you think I would be surprised to learn about you?

_____

_____

_____

_____

_____

_____

_____

_____

_____

_____

_____

_____

_____

_____

# Are there any songs that always make you feel better?

_____

_____

_____

_____

_____

_____

_____

_____

_____

_____

_____

_____

_____

_____

_____

# What is something you learned later in life that you wish you'd learned earlier?

_____

_____

_____

_____

_____

_____

_____

_____

_____

_____

_____

_____

_____

_____

_____

_____

**Is the present anything like you imagined
the future would be when you were a kid?
How is it different or the same?**

_____

_____

_____

_____

_____

_____

_____

_____

_____

_____

_____

_____

_____

_____

_____

_____

# Do you have any favorite quotes?

You zoom eighty years into the future and
encounter your great great great grandchild.
What qualities do you most hope they possess?

_____

_____

_____

_____

_____

_____

_____

_____

_____

_____

_____

_____

_____

_____

_____

_____

_____

# What are some keys to living a good life?

_____

_____

_____

_____

_____

_____

_____

_____

_____

_____

_____

_____

_____

_____

# How do you define success?

_____

_____

_____

_____

_____

_____

_____

_____

_____

_____

_____

_____

_____

_____

_____

_____

_____

_____

# Life's Tough Moments

# What is one of the toughest decisions you've ever had to make?

_____

_____

_____

_____

_____

_____

_____

_____

_____

_____

_____

_____

_____

_____

_____

_____

_____

## What advice would you give me when I am confused and don't know what path to take?

_____

_____

_____

_____

_____

_____

_____

_____

_____

_____

_____

_____

_____

_____

_____

_____

# What is the first thing you do when you are really afraid?

_____

_____

_____

_____

_____

_____

_____

_____

_____

_____

_____

_____

_____

_____

_____

_____

## What is one of your most difficult experiences? How did you make it through?

_____

_____

_____

_____

_____

_____

_____

_____

_____

_____

_____

_____

_____

_____

_____

_____

**Was there a particularly challenging phase of your life? How did you cope during that time?**

_____

_____

_____

_____

_____

_____

_____

_____

_____

_____

_____

_____

_____

_____

_____

_____

# What difficult experience are you now extremely grateful for?

_____

_____

_____

_____

_____

_____

_____

_____

_____

_____

_____

_____

_____

_____

_____

# How do you handle major disappointment?

# On Saying Goodbye

# What was a difficult goodbye of your life? How did it change you?

_____

_____

_____

_____

_____

_____

_____

_____

_____

_____

_____

_____

_____

_____

_____

_____

## What do you think happens when we die? What do you hope happens?

_____

_____

_____

_____

_____

_____

_____

_____

_____

_____

_____

_____

_____

_____

_____

_____

**When you are gone, what is something you will want me to remember you telling me?**

_____

_____

_____

_____

_____

_____

_____

_____

_____

_____

_____

_____

_____

_____

_____

_____

**Is there a tradition of ours that you hope
I will continue? If we don't have any,
is there one that you'd like to start?**

_____

_____

_____

_____

_____

_____

_____

_____

_____

_____

_____

_____

_____

_____

# When you are gone, how do you hope to be remembered?

_____

_____

_____

_____

_____

_____

_____

_____

_____

_____

_____

_____

_____

_____

_____

## If you could choose your last words to me, what would they be?

_____

_____

_____

_____

_____

_____

_____

_____

_____

_____

_____

_____

_____

_____

# Additional Questions
# to Each Other

**Use these pages to fill in any additional questions, answers, or notes to each other**

_____

_____

_____

_____

_____

_____

_____

_____

_____

_____

_____

_____

_____

_____

_____

_____

_____

_____

_____

# About the Author

Melissa Pennel is a writer, mother, and author of the "Questions You'll Wish You Asked" series of journals. After losing all parents and grandparents by the age of thirty, she began urging everyone to ask their family questions and write down their answers—this journal series was born of that mission.

To find more of Melissa's work on how to live a full and authentic life, go to FollowYourFireCoaching.com.

*This journal is in memory of her grandparents.*